MW01485274

Topographic Maps!

Its Uses in Understanding Elevation, Slopes and Relief and Interpretation

Grade 6-8 Earth Science

BABY PROFESSOR
EDUCATION KIDS

First Edition, 2024

Published in the United States by Speedy Publishing LLC, 40 E Main Street, Newark, Delaware 19711 USA.

© 2024 Baby Professor Books, an imprint of Speedy Publishing LLC

All images in this book have been reproduced with the knowledge and prior consent of the artists concerned, and no responsibility is accepted by producer, publisher, or printer for any infringement of copyright or otherwise arising from the contents of this publication.

Baby Professor Books are available at special discounts when purchased in bulk for industrial and sales-promotional use. For details contact our Special Sales Team at Speedy Publishing LLC, 40 E Main Street, Newark, Delaware 19711 USA. Telephone (888) 248-4521 Fax: (210) 519-4043.

10 9 8 7 6 * 5 4 3 2 1

Print Edition: 9781541990418
Digital Edition: 9781541991774
Hardcover Edition: 9781541989375

See the world in pictures. Build your knowledge in style.
www.speedypublishing.com

Table of Contents

Chapter One:
Uses of Topographic Maps. 7

Chapter Two:
How Land Features are Shown on
Topographic Maps 33

Chapter Three:
More About Contour Lines. 51

Summary 67

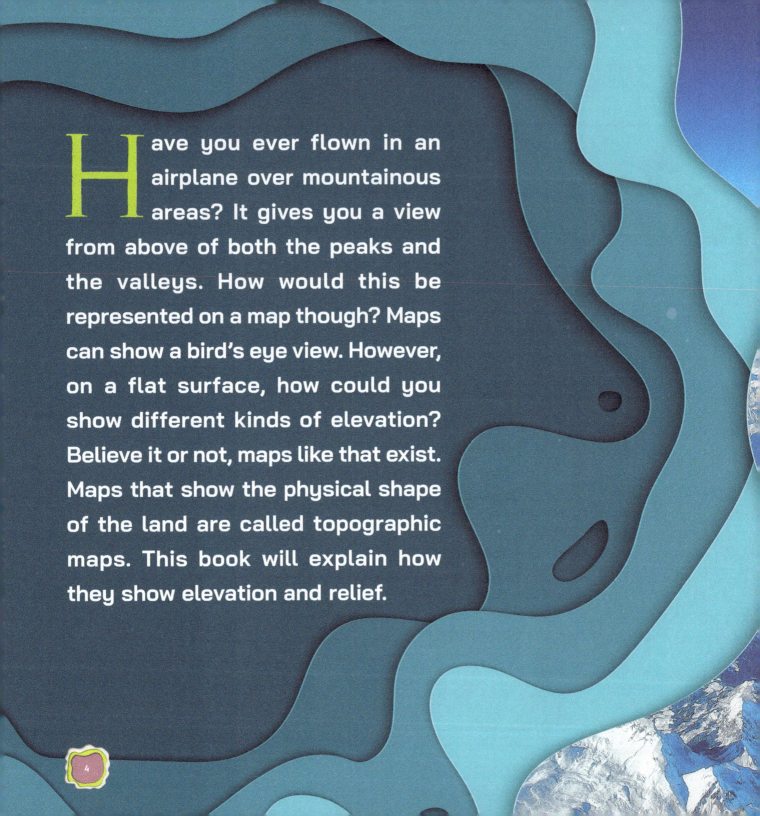

Have you ever flown in an airplane over mountainous areas? It gives you a view from above of both the peaks and the valleys. How would this be represented on a map though? Maps can show a bird's eye view. However, on a flat surface, how could you show different kinds of elevation? Believe it or not, maps like that exist. Maps that show the physical shape of the land are called topographic maps. This book will explain how they show elevation and relief.

Flying in an airplane over mountainous areas gives a view from above of both the peaks and the valleys.

Chapter One:
Uses of Topographic Maps

Topographic maps show features on the Earth's surface, both man-made and natural. Topographic maps can use symbols to show land and structures as they would look from above. These include things like swamps or marshes. In addition to that, topographic maps will show information on elevation, <u>relief</u>, and slopes.

Topographic maps are maps which show features on the Earth's surface.

People convert aerial photographs into maps, then they add color, shading, and symbols, and other necessary details.

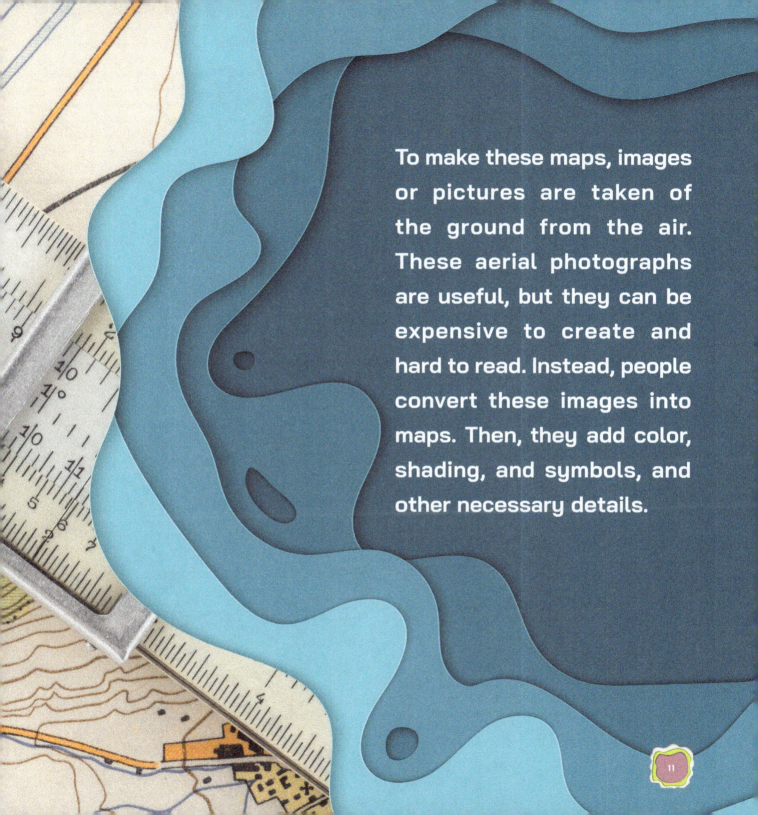

To make these maps, images or pictures are taken of the ground from the air. These aerial photographs are useful, but they can be expensive to create and hard to read. Instead, people convert these images into maps. Then, they add color, shading, and symbols, and other necessary details.

Types of Maps:

There are many kinds of maps. They can generally be split into two categories. There are reference maps and there are thematic maps. Reference maps show definite locations, structures, boundaries, or features. These are the maps you could look at to show you towns, cities, roads, mountains, state boundaries, bodies of water, or even time zones. The information on reference maps do not typically change quickly or easily. Topographic maps are reference maps.

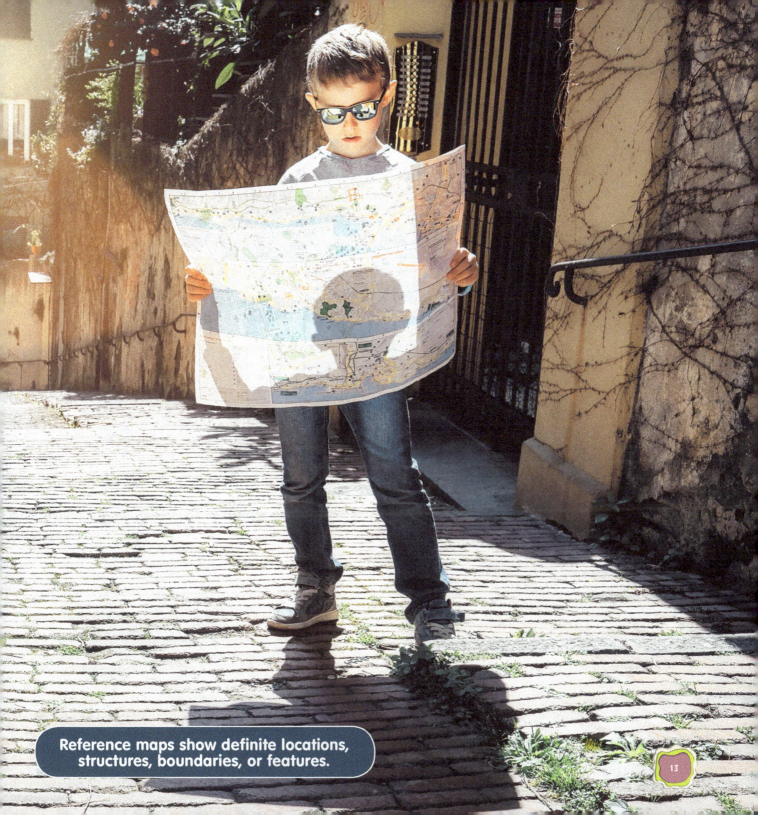

Reference maps show definite locations, structures, boundaries, or features.

Election result USA 2020
The winning Electoral Votes

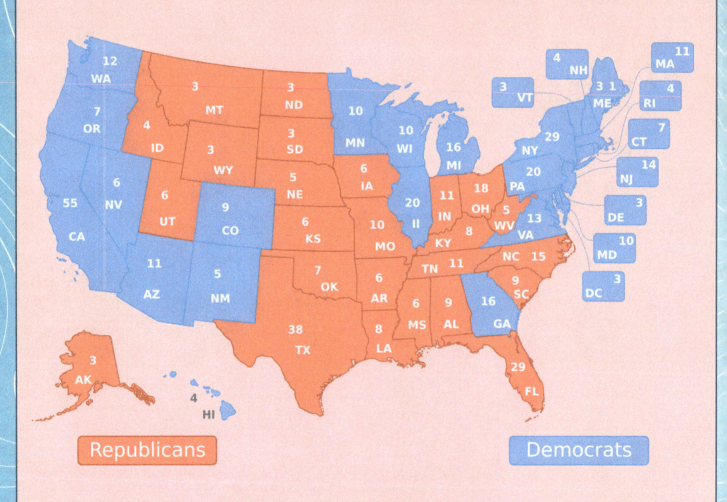

Republicans

Democrats

Thematic maps have additional information like election results.

Thematic maps show the basic information that might be on a reference map. Then, they add additional information. These are things like weather systems, population sizes, natural resources, or election results. Usually, these maps have information that can easily change and must be updated often.

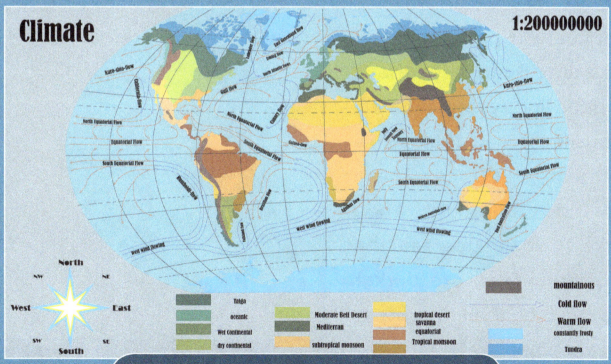

Climate 1:200000000

Taiga
oceanic
Wet continental
dry continental

Moderate Belt Desert
Mediterran
subtropical monsoon

tropical desert
savanna
equaforial
Tropical monsoon

mountainous
Cold flow
Warm flow
constantly frosty
Tundra

North
NW NE
West East
SW SE
South

Thematic maps maps have information that can easily change and must be updated often.

How do Topographic Maps Show Elevation, Relief, and Slopes?

Topographic maps tell us about the elevation, relief, and slopes of the land using <u>contour</u> lines. These are lines that connect points of equal elevation. Sometimes these contour lines are numbered. They might say things like 450 feet or 500 feet. These are index contours. They make it easier to read the elevation. They are darker and thicker than the other contour lines.

16

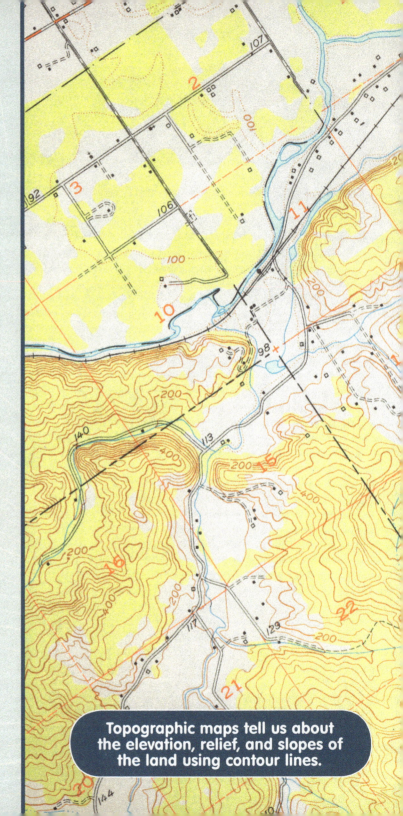

Topographic maps tell us about the elevation, relief, and slopes of the land using contour lines.

Index contours tend to appear at regular intervals, for example at every 50 feet. The difference of elevation between each contour line is called the contour interval. Interval means the time or space between things.

The difference of elevation between each contour line is called the contour interval.

Footbridge

Uses of Topographic Maps:

Topographic maps have various uses. In geology, topographic maps are used to find key surface features and landforms. They can also be used to find the slope in a certain area. This can help <u>geologists</u> predict things like the flow of water, and even potential mudslides or landslides.

18

In geology, topographic maps are used to find key surface features and landforms.

19

Engineers will study topographic maps before building roads or erecting buildings.

Engineers also need to be aware of the flow of water before beginning certain construction projects. They will study topographic maps before building roads or erecting buildings.

Another use of topographic maps is for business. Business owners can look at a topographic map to determine where they might build new factories or stores. Government organizations do something similar when they are looking to construct new buildings for the public.

Business owners can look at a topographic map to determine where they might build new factories or stores.

People can look at topographic maps to plan where to go hiking.

Finally, topographic maps can be used for recreation. People can look at these maps to plan where to go hiking, biking, backpacking, or camping. If you want a challenge, you might want steeper hills. If not, you might want lower areas of elevation.

Some people might also use these maps for geocaching. This is when people use coordinates to find hidden objects. It is a bit like modern day treasure hunting with <u>GPS</u>.

Some people might also use topographic maps for geocaching.

Statue of the Greek God Atlas holding the globe on his shoulders.

Atlases:

An atlas is a collection of maps that are published together. It is named after the titan, Atlas, from Greek myth. He was punished by having to carry the weight of the sky on his shoulders.

Atlases can be varying in size.

Atlases can be varying in size. Some are small enough to be pocket sized. Others are massive enough you would need a stand to support it! These atlases are meant to present all the geographic facts of the world.

A good atlas would have about a hundred or more maps. Usually they start with the whole world, and then have more specific maps for continents, then countries, then cities and so on. The index provided would help locate the necessary maps quickly.

A good atlas would have about a hundred or more maps.

Atlases are important tools for geologists and engineers. It gives them a lot of information on a specific location. Different maps show different things which can help give them a better understanding. This is important since maps make three-dimensional things two-dimensional. This means there will be a certain level of distortion.

Atlases are important tools for geologists and engineers.

Chapter Two:
How Land Features are Shown on Topographic Maps

In order to read a topographic map, or any map, you need to be familiar with the symbols.

In order to read a topographic map, or any map, you need to be familiar with the symbols. Fortunately, most maps will have a key or a legend to explain what they mean. Common symbols include schools, churches, camping sites, picnic areas, roads, and railroad tracks.

Symbols:

Typically in the United States, black or red lines will symbolize roads. The larger the road, the wider and darker the line might be. Lines that are tick-marked are for railroads. Circles or stars represent cities. Natural formations, like swamps and rivers, will also get their own symbols.

Typically in the United States, black or red lines will symbolize roads.

700

800

•950

37

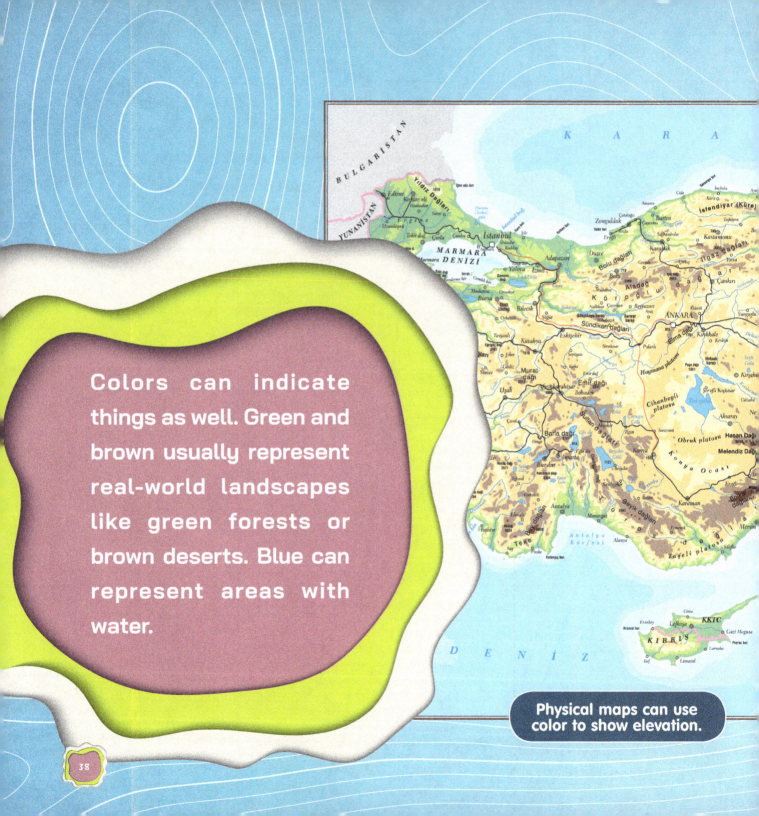

Colors can indicate things as well. Green and brown usually represent real-world landscapes like green forests or brown deserts. Blue can represent areas with water.

Physical maps can use color to show elevation.

Colors can get confusing though, so it is always good to check the legend. Physical maps can use color to show elevation. Green can be used to indicate lower levels of elevation. Darker colors might be used to show higher levels of elevation.

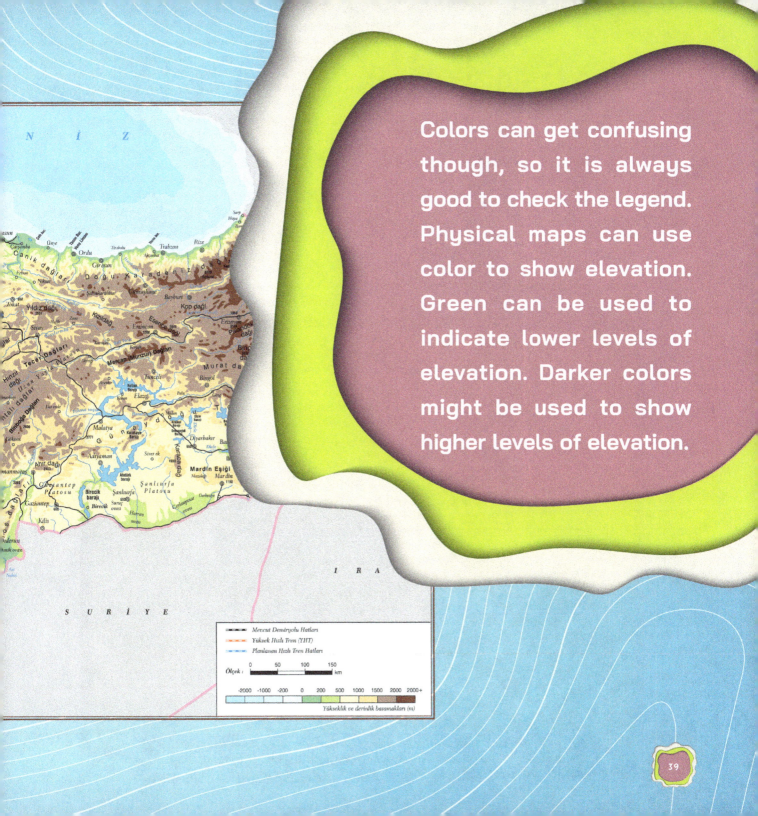

Map Scales:

Scale shows the relationship between distance on a map and what that distance would be in real-life on the ground. Every map should have a scale shown at the bottom. This helps people get a rough idea of what the distance is between two points.

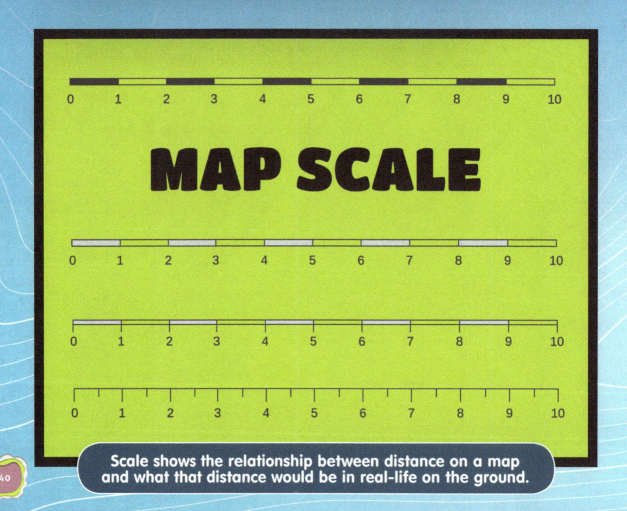

Scale shows the relationship between distance on a map and what that distance would be in real-life on the ground.

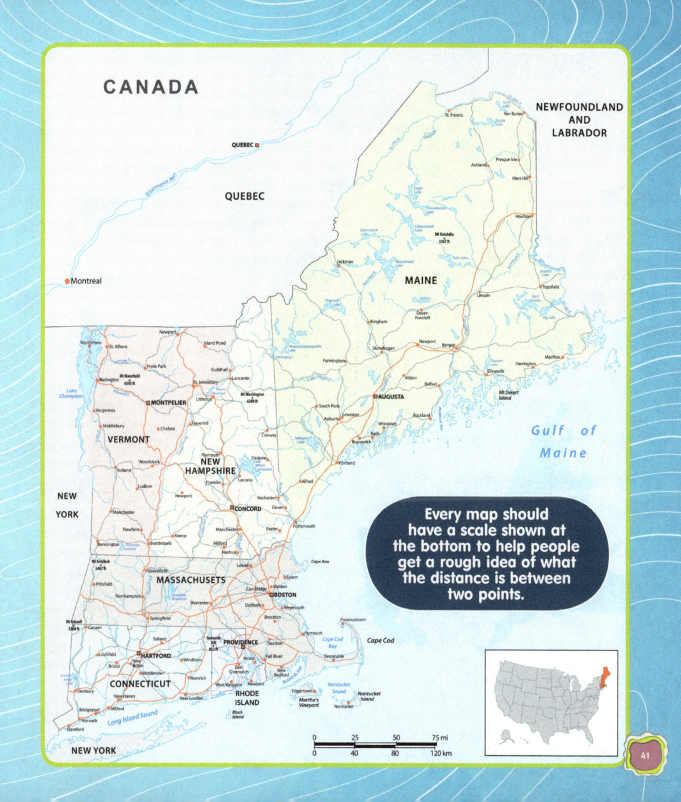

CANADA

NEWFOUNDLAND
AND
LABRADOR

QUEBEC

QUEBEC

St. Francis

Van Buren

Ashland

Presque Isle

Mars Hill

Montreal

Houlton

MAINE

Mt Katahdin
5267 ft

Jackman

Lincoln

Topsfield

Newport

Bangor

Harrington

Machias

Bingham

Dover-
Foxcroft

Ellsworth

Skowhegan

Farmington

Albion

Belfast

Mt Desert
Island

Newport

North Hero

Island Pond

AUGUSTA

St. Albans

Guildhall

Lancaster

South Paris

Lewiston

Wiscasset

Rockland

Gulf of
Maine

Hyde Park

St. Johnsbury

Auburn

Burlington

Mt Mansfield
4393 ft

Littleton

Mt Washington
6288 ft

Bath

Lake
Champlain

Haverhill

Brunswick

MONTPELIER

Vergennes

Chelsea

Conway

Middlebury

Sebago
Lake

VERMONT

Plymouth

Ossipee

Portland

Woodstock

NEW
HAMPSHIRE

Rutland

Franklin

Laconia

Alfred

Ludlow

Newport

Rochester

NEW
YORK

Manchester

Dover

CONCORD

Newfane

Manchester

Portsmouth

Bennington

Brattleboro

Keene

Milford

Exeter

Nashua

Mt Greylock
3487 ft

Cape Ann

Greenfield

Lowell

Pittsfield

Salem

Northampton

Melden

MASSACHUSETS

Cambridge

BOSTON

Worcester

Dedham

Weymouth

Springfield

Brockton

Mt Frissell
2380 ft

Canaan

Plymouth

Provincetown

Cape Cod
Bay

Cape Cod

Tolland

Jerimoth
Hill
812 ft

PROVIDENCE

Taunton

Litchfield

HARTFORD

Windham

Bristol

Fall River

Barnstable

New
Britain

East
Greenwich

New
Bedford

Bristol

Middletown

Norwich

West Kingston

Newport

Edgartown

Nantucket
Sound

Nantucket
Island

CONNECTICUT

New Haven

New London

RHODE
ISLAND

Martha's
Vineyard

Nantucket

Danbury

Block
Island

Bridgeport

Milford

Norwalk

Stamford

Long Island Sound

NEW YORK

> Every map should
> have a scale shown at
> the bottom to help people
> get a rough idea of what
> the distance is between
> two points.

| 0 | 25 | 50 | 75 mi |
| 0 | 40 | 80 | 120 km |

41

Cartographers, or mapmakers, can show scale in two main ways. One is as a ratio. For example, 1:24,000 or 1 to 24,000 is a ratio. This means that one inch on the map would equal 24,000 inches in real life on the ground. 24,000 inches would equal 2,000 feet. That is slightly less than half a mile.

Cartographers, or mapmakers, can show scale in two main ways.

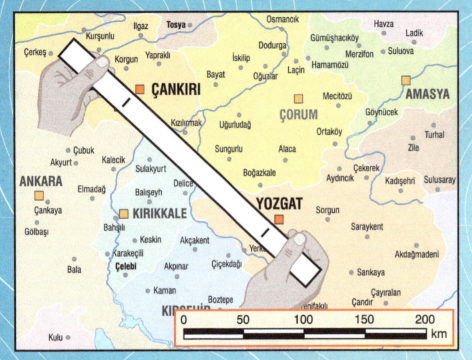

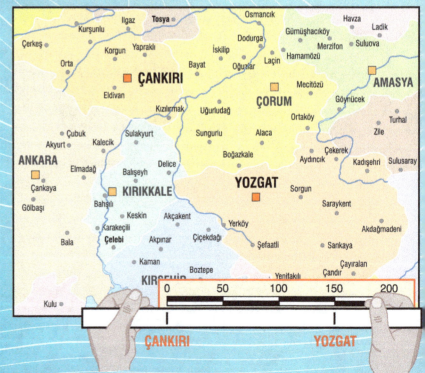

ÇANKIRI   YOZGAT

Other than ratios, a map might use a scale bar. These allow you to measure the length of a segment of line and compare it to a distance on the map. Maps can have multiple scale bars. Some will show <u>metric</u> distances. Another bar might show the distance in miles. Some bars could demonstrate the distance in feet.

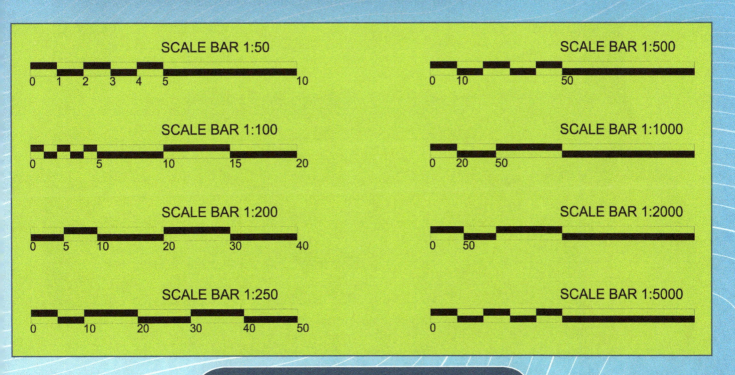

A scale bar allows you to measure the length of a segment of line and compare it to a distance on the map.

A compass rose is used to show the basic directions of north, west, south, and east.

The Cardinal Directions:

Maps will usually have a symbol called a compass rose. This is used to show the cardinal directions. These are the basic directions of north, west, south, and east. These are the same as you would see on a compass. If there is no compass rose on a map, it is standard to assume that north is at the top. This might not always be the case though.

North and south are formed from the imaginary line called an axis. It is around this line that the Earth spins. The top of this axis is the North Pole. The bottom is the South Pole.

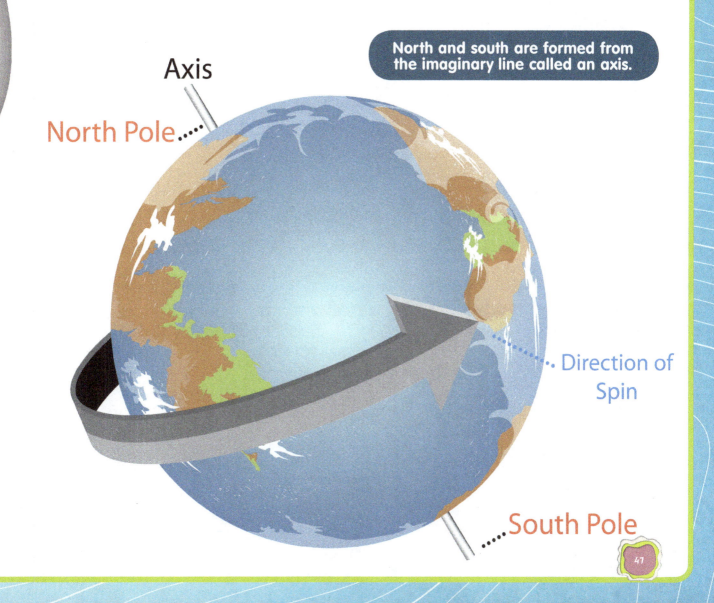

Axis

North Pole

North and south are formed from the imaginary line called an axis.

Direction of Spin

South Pole

The Sun rises in the East and sets in the West.

48

East and west are also related to how the Earth spins. East is the direction that the Earth turns towards. West is the direction that it turns from. That is why the Sun rises in the East and sets in the West. Unlike north and south, east and west do not have a definite location. You could circle around the globe as many times as you like going east or west and never arrive anywhere!

Chapter Three: More About Contour Lines

We learned about contour lines in the first chapter. It shows the elevation between two places. For instance, if you begin on a hill at 500 feet elevation and drive down to 450 feet elevation, the contour line will show the slope downhill and the relief is about 50 feet. You can know the relief is about 50 feet by counting the contour lines. If there are five, and each one represents 10 feet, you can multiply to get the answer. This chapter will explain about how contour lines work in fuller detail.

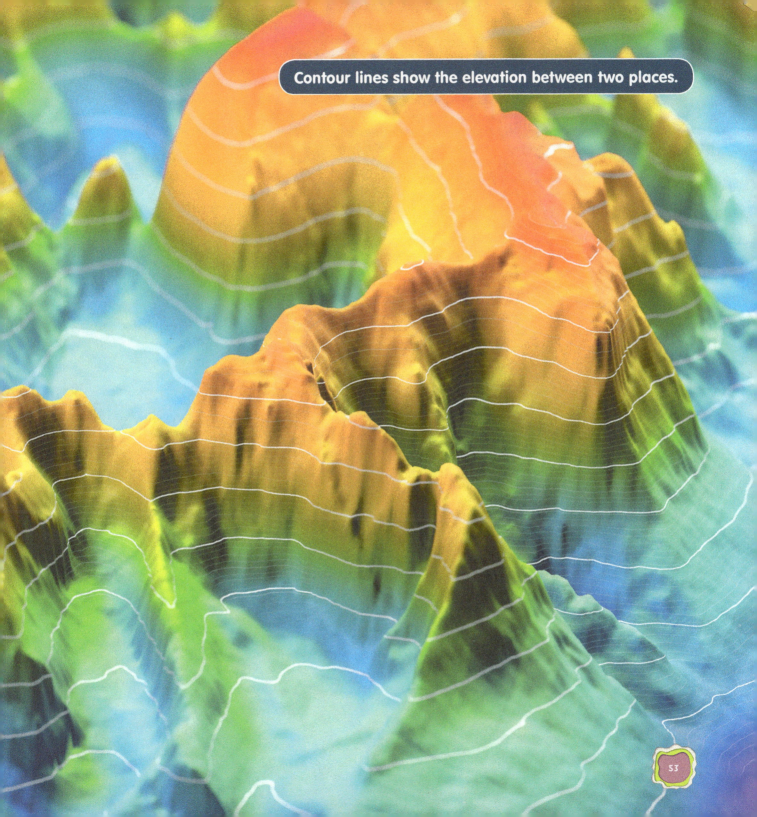

Contour lines show the elevation between two places.

53

In some places on a topographic map, contour lines are closer together or there is a larger distance between the lines.

Slope and Distance Between Contour Lines:

In some places on a topographic map, you may notice that the contour lines are closer together. In other places, there is a larger distance between the lines. This is how you know which slopes are steeper. If you go from 500 feet to 450 feet, that is a sharp decline. There is not much distance for that drop, so the lines will be closer. On the other hand, if you drop 50 feet over a long trip, the contour lines will have more distance between them.

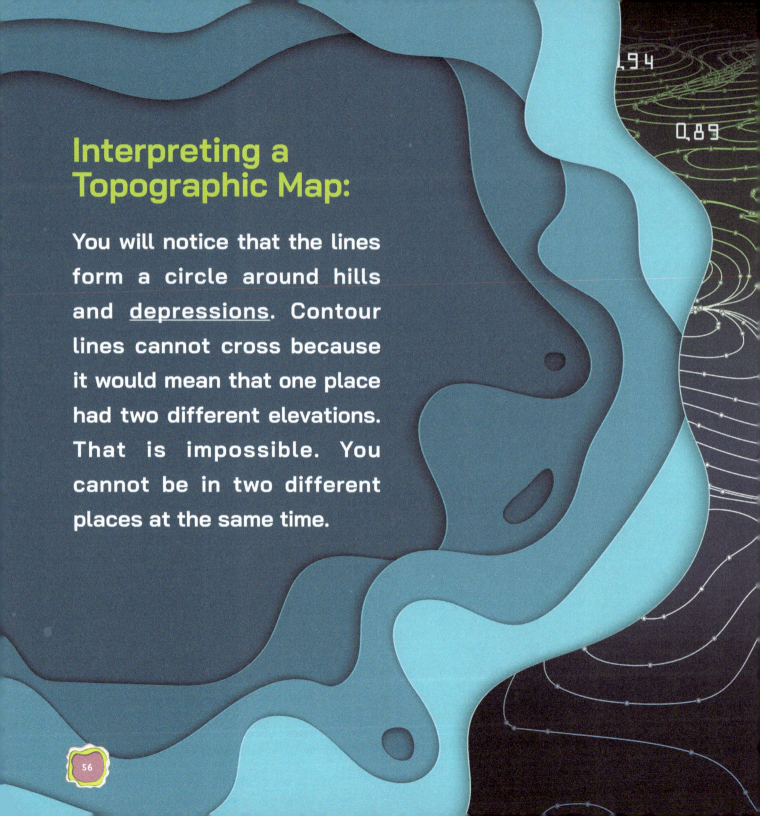

Interpreting a Topographic Map:

You will notice that the lines form a circle around hills and depressions. Contour lines cannot cross because it would mean that one place had two different elevations. That is impossible. You cannot be in two different places at the same time.

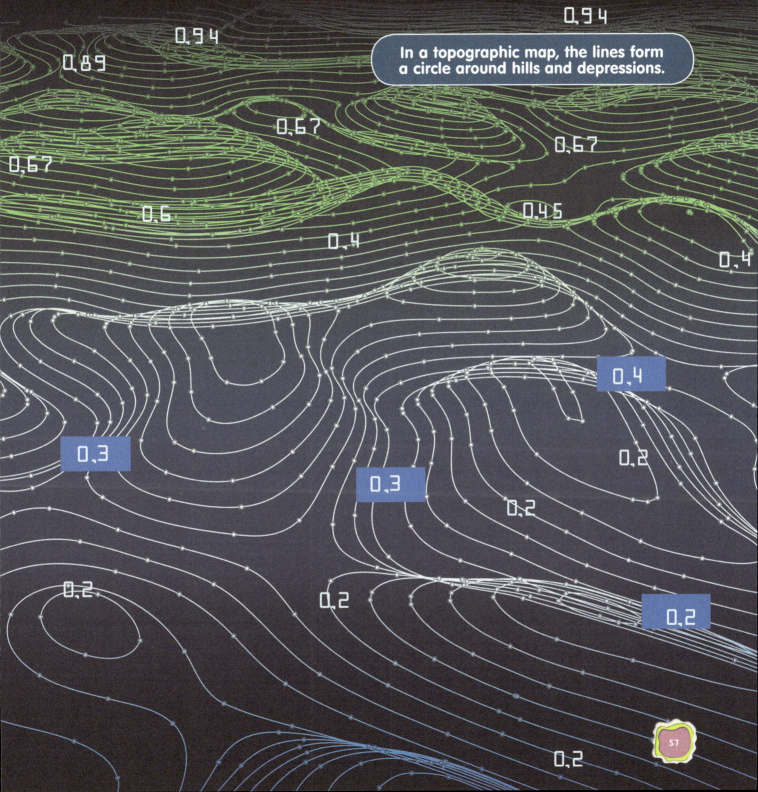

0,94

0,94

0,89

In a topographic map, the lines form
a circle around hills and depressions.

0,67

0,67

0,67

0,6

0,45

0,4

0,4

0,4

0,3

0,2

0,3

0,2

0,2

0,2

0,2

0,2

57

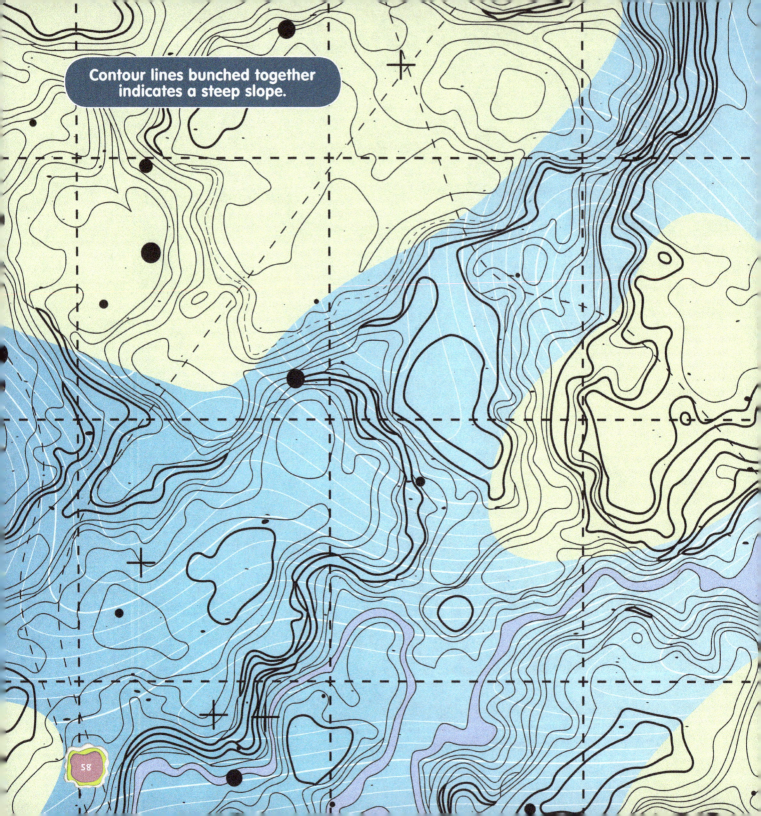

Contour lines bunched together indicates a steep slope.

58

Contour lines show how shallow or steep the elevation is. The symbols will help interpret what that might look like. For instance, you might see contour lines bunched together. This indicates a steep slope. Then you see a red triangle. This represents a mountain. That makes sense as mountains have high elevation and high relief.

Perhaps you see a river on a topographic map. It is surrounded by large white areas that are flat. What does this mean? It is likely you are looking at a floodplain. You should also note that the river will be flowing from a higher elevation to a lower one.

A hiker navigating with a topographic map.

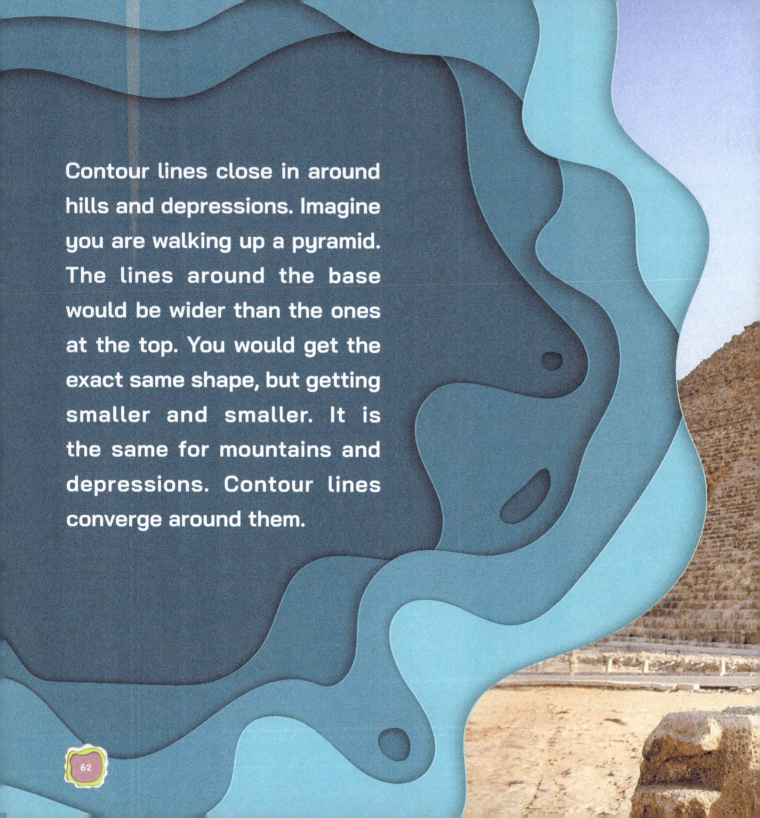

Contour lines close in around hills and depressions. Imagine you are walking up a pyramid. The lines around the base would be wider than the ones at the top. You would get the exact same shape, but getting smaller and smaller. It is the same for mountains and depressions. Contour lines converge around them.

The contour lines around the base of a pyramid would be wider than the ones at the top.

63

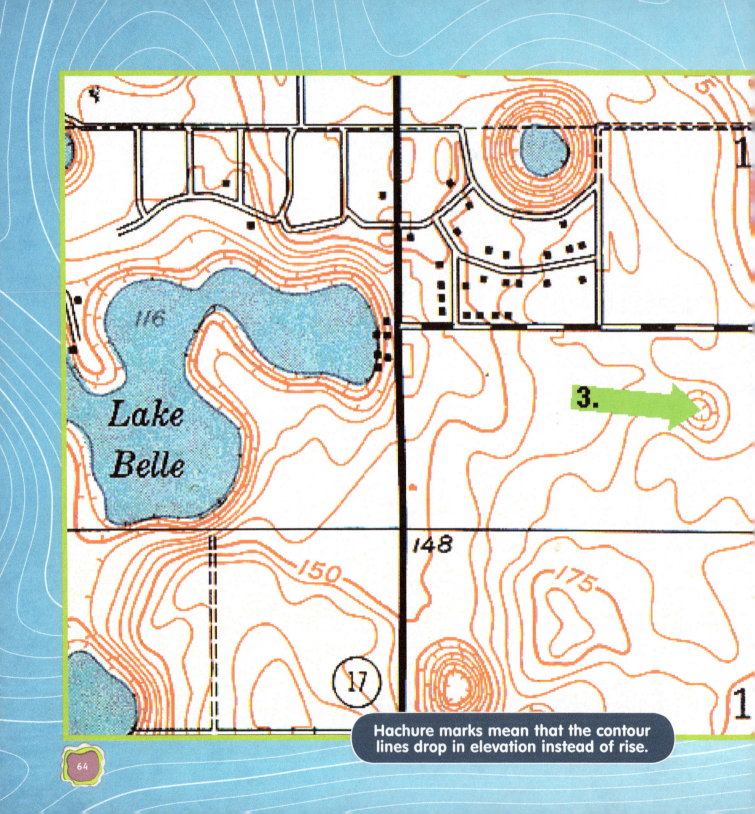

116

Lake
Belle

3.

148

150

175

17

1

1

Hachure marks mean that the contour lines drop in elevation instead of rise.

64

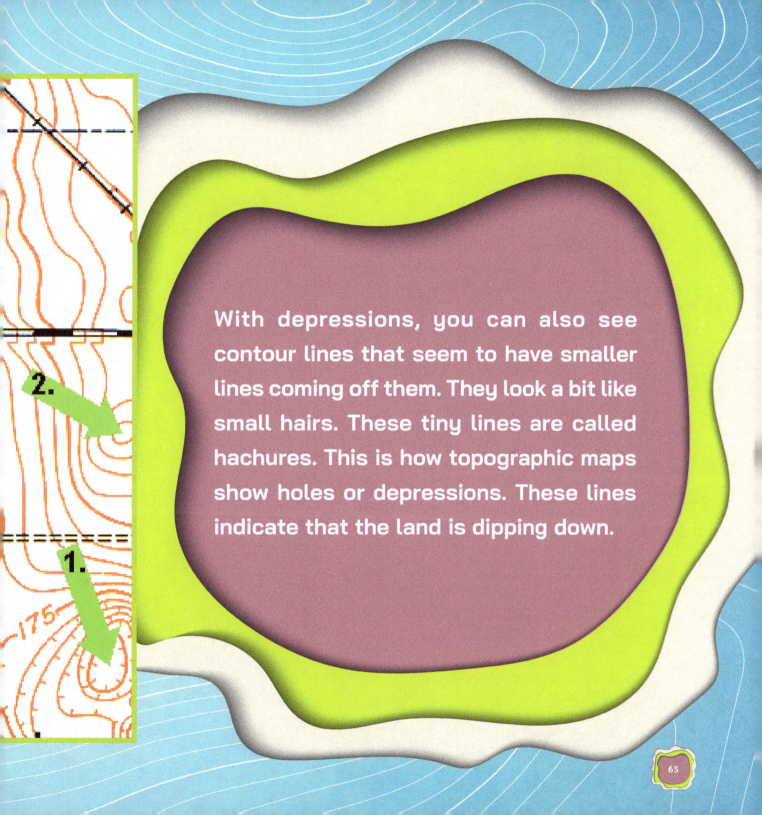

With depressions, you can also see contour lines that seem to have smaller lines coming off them. They look a bit like small hairs. These tiny lines are called hachures. This is how topographic maps show holes or depressions. These lines indicate that the land is dipping down.

Summary

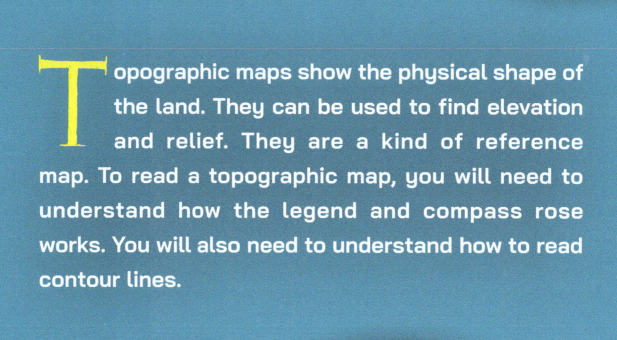

Topographic maps show the physical shape of the land. They can be used to find elevation and relief. They are a kind of reference map. To read a topographic map, you will need to understand how the legend and compass rose works. You will also need to understand how to read contour lines.

These lines show areas of the same elevation. The closer the lines are to each other, the steeper that area is. Conversely, the farther apart they are, the less the land slopes. As a result, contour lines converge around mountains and depressions. Hachures can also indicate depressions. Index contours and interval contours help show the exact amount of elevation.

Glossary

Contour (pg. 16): an outline, especially one that represents the shape or boundary of something.

Depression (pg. 56): a hollow place

Geologist (pg. 18): someone who studies Geology which is the study of the Earth and its history.

GPS (pg. 24): This stands for Global Positioning System. This is a navigation system that works using data collected by satellites.

Metric (pg. 45): This system of measurement uses meters and kilometers.

Relief (pg. 8): the differences in elevation of land surfaces

Visit

www.speedypublishing.com

To view and download free content on your
favorite subject and browse our catalog of new
and exciting books for readers of all ages.